STARS

Mojisola Adebayo

With illustrations by Candice Purwin

methuen | drama

LONDON · NEW YORK · OXFORD · NEW DELHI · SYDNEY

METHUEN DRAMA
Bloomsbury Publishing Plc
50 Bedford Square, London, WC1B 3DP, UK
1385 Broadway, New York, NY 10018, USA
29 Earlsfort Terrace, Dublin 2, Ireland

BLOOMSBURY, METHUEN DRAMA and the Methuen
Drama logo are trademarks of Bloomsbury Publishing Plc

First published in Great Britain 2023

A catalogue record for this book is available from the British Library.

A catalog record for this book is available from the Library of Congress.

ISBN: PB: 978-1-3504-1100-5
ePDF: 978-1-3504-1101-2
eBook: 978-1-3504-1102-9

Series: Modern Plays

Typeset by Mark Heslington Ltd, Scarborough, North Yorkshire

To find out more about our authors and books visit
www.bloomsbury.com and sign up for our newsletters.

A **TAMASHA** AND **INSTITUTE OF CONTEMPORARY ARTS**
CO-PRODUCTION

STARS

An Afrofuturist Space Odyssey

By Mojisola Adebayo

Supported using public funding by

**ARTS COUNCIL
ENGLAND**

ABOUT THE WRITER

Mojisola Adebayo (BA, MA, PhD, FRSL, FHEA) is a playwright, performer, director, producer, mentor, workshop facilitator and teacher who has been making theatre for social change, internationally, for over thirty years, from Antarctica to Zimbabwe. Mojisola's own plays include *Moj of the Antarctic: An African Odyssey* (Lyric Hammersmith), *Muhammad Ali and Me* (Ovalhouse), *48 Minutes for Palestine/ Oranges and Stones* (Ashtar Theatre, Ramallah), *Desert Boy* (Nitro/ Albany Theatre), *The Listeners* (Pegasus Theatre), *I Stand Corrected* (Artscape, Cape Town), *The Interrogation of Sandra Bland* (Bush Theatre), *Wind/Rush Generation(s)* (National Theatre: Connections), *Nothello* (Coventry Belgrade Theatre) and *Family Tree* (Actors Touring Company/Belgrade Theatre/Brixton House), which won the Alfred Fagon Award for Best Play of 2021 and tours nationally from March 2023. Publications include *Mojisola Adebayo: Plays One* and *Plays Two*, *The Theatre for Development Handbook*, co-written with John Martin and Manisha Mehta and *Black British Queer Plays and Practitioners*: *An Anthology of Afriquia Theatre*, co-edited with Lynette Goddard (Methuen Drama). Mojisola teaches at Queen Mary University of London, is an Associate Artist of Black Lives Black Words, AICRE, Pan Arts, the Building the Anti-Racist Classroom collective and an Honorary Fellow of Rose Bruford College. At the time of writing, Mojisola is on a research fellowship at the University of Potsdam, Germany and is a Writer-on-Attachment to the National Theatre (UK). *STARS* (Tamasha Theatre Company/Institute of Contemporary Arts) was developed on a residency with idle women, shortlisted for the George Devine Award 2022 and premieres at ICA London in April 2023, before a national tour. See mojisolaadebayo. co.uk for more.

ACKNOWLEDGEMENTS FROM THE WRITER

I conceived *STARS* during an artist's residency with idle women in the summer of 2016, with research and development processes and staged readings at Ovalhouse Theatre Downstairs, Homotopia Festival and online. The project was developed with the support of Arts Council England and Queen Mary University of London Centre for Public Engagement and the School of English and Drama. Thank you to all the individuals at these organisations who enabled the play to be written and finally produced, including Rachel Anderson and Cis O'Boyle of idle women; Stella Kanu and Owen Calvert-Lyons of Ovalhouse; Alex Ferguson and Char Binns of Homotopia; Justin Hunt of ACE; Professors Caoimhe McAvinchey, Catherine Silverstone and Dominic Johnson of QMUL; Debo Adebayo, Fin Kennedy, Pooja Ghai, Valerie Synmoie, Rema Chandran and everyone at Tamasha theatre company; the folks at ICA who said yes including Leila Hasham, Kiera Blakey, Bengi Ünsa, Rosalie Doubal, Ifeanyi Awachie, Nydia A. Swaby, Sara Sassenelli and Natasha Chubbuck as well as all the workers duly credited in the programme – thank you! Thank you to Kieran Enticknap and also Hannah Miller for her casting support and advice.

A big thanks also to all of the arts workers, audience members, workshop participants and mentees who were integral to the *STARS* research and development processes in 2016, 2018 and 2021, including: Candice Purwin and all the participants at Accrington women's centre and aboard the *Selina Cooper* in the summer of 2016; Valentino Vecchietti of Intersex Equality Rights; Rasha Farah, Mary Otuko and Kabung Lomodong of FORWARD; S. Ama Wray, Rajha Shakiry, Debo Adebayo, Claudine Rousseau, Pablo Fernández Baz, Andrea Ainsworth, Alison Pottinger; Jodi Bickerton, Jenny Sealey and Mette Philipsen of Graeae; Natalie Cooper, Sonny Nwachukwu, Dike Okoh, Lettie Precious, Conrad Kira, Karen Tomlin; Dave Wright and Jules Deering at QMUL; Franc Ashman, Rikki Beadle-Blair, Jacqui Beckford, Izegbuwa Oleghe; Matthew Xia, Martina Laird, Nao Nagai, Stephen Lloyd, Gurpreet Singh, Yvonne Beckford, Stephen Collins, Tallulah Frendo, Ashlee Roberts, Awa Jagne, Dominique Sotuminu and Sue Mayo. Thank you to Gail Babb, Miriam Nabarro, Gillian Tan, Dawn Estefan, Shanika Warren-Markland, James Dawson, Stuart Glover, Maariyha Sharjil, Debra Michaels, Bradley Charles and all the ICA workshop participants for coming aboard for this premiere production. We did it!

Thanks to those who have previously published either versions of or extracts from *STARS*, including James Hogan of Oberon Books; Isabel Waidner and Dostoyevsky Wannabe; John R. Gordon and Rikki Beadle-Blair of Team Angelica; Dean Atta and Wasafiri; Serena Grasso and Dom O'Hanlon at Methuen Drama as well as Callan McCarthy and Alexandra Betkowska.

I also want to extend a personal thank you to friends (who are not already named above) who came to see *STARS* in process, who listened and gave me feedback, supported me in dealing with the issues raised by the play or simply inspired me to keep going, perhaps without realising it. Thank you to Sarah Ives, Sandra Vacciana, Carole Jones, Lennox Goddard, Nicky Bashall, Stella Barnes, Rita Das, Paul Woodward, Topher Campbell, Del LaGrace Volcano, Kay Soord, Hilary Marshall, Antonia Kemi Coker, Katy Forkha, Deni Francis, Crin Claxton, Nadia Atia, Kate Lowry, Ellie Beedham, Tariq Alvi, Anna Wallbank, Kumar Muniandy, Ola Aminashawun, Stewart Pringle, Anna Napier, Charlie Folorunsho, Anja Sunhyun Michaelsen and Sadhvi Dar. In loving memory and thanks to Solange Rousseau. An immense thanks to my extraordinary therapist. Thank you ever to Nicole Wolf and 'unser' Umar.

WRITER'S NOTE

I've been wondering about my lost orgasm – where did it go? Outer space?! After years of therapy I can laugh about it but as a survivor of sexual abuse and gender-based violence, it's still a very tough question. So, when one summer idle women invited me to float on a Lancashire boat, the *Selina Cooper*, relax along canals and write a play, I laid back and thought, well, it's not just me, lots of people struggle with sex and *millions* of women all over the world are cut off from the possibility of pleasure, because they go through harmful traditional surgeries as girls known as FGM. I connected with FORWARD, a fantastic charity led by African women, and learnt a lot about FGM from them. I'm also part of the LGBTIQA+ community and dialogues with Valentino Vecchietti of Intersex Equality Rights creatively informed my writing. Vecchietti and artist/activist Del LaGrace Volcano taught me about non-consensual surgeries faced by many intersex children here in Britain. However, FGM and childhood intersex surgeries are rarely discussed on the same page and the I on the end of LGBTQI is often forgotten. But, I thought, these issues have the same root. I decided to connect these questions of the gender binary and control, in one story exploring the politics of pleasure. I read copiously and ran workshops onboard the *Selina Cooper*. I met the magical artist Candice Purwin on the idle women's boat too, and her amazing drawings are woven through the show which becomes an Afrofuturist space odyssey.

Some people might ask, why space travel and Afrofuturism in a play that seeks healing from sexual trauma? The idea came from my need to create some emotional distance for myself while dealing with painful subject matter and wanting to find sensorial joy through it all. I thought, make the central character much older than you are now and take the story out of this world. That's how I came up with the premise of an old lady who wants to go into space in search of her own orgasm. I then asked, how can I look at these themes through a beautiful Black lens? My quest led me to the extraordinary astronomy, mythology and visual culture of the Dogon peoples of Mali, West Africa which inspired many of Candice's illustrations. My collaborator-brother-friend DJ Debo and I started talking music and came up with the idea of creating 'a concept album for the stage'. As a performer, I started exploring movement possibilities with my long-time collaborator-sista-friend S. Ama Wray and, together with lots of people in the research and development processes from 2016 to now (all named above), we found ourselves here!

We knew from the start that we wanted not just the content but the form of the show to be uplifting, releasing and healing – not just a play but an event. I have often felt frustrated that theatres are dead spaces after 11 pm – just when we could get a party started! Debo and I came up with this idea of a play that can transform into a club night, starting with a DJ mixing music all the way through the show. That ecstatic feeling of being on a dance floor with your friends around you – that's almost orgasmic for me – the earth moves! The club night also features insights from women who've been exploring the politics of pleasure in workshops at the ICA. Thanks to them!

Indeed, there are so many who have been involved in this project and I am immensely grateful to all the inspirational people who inspired, supported, developed and created *STARS*. They are duly acknowledged here but I also want to take this space to express my strange gratitude to all the theatre programmers who rejected *STARS*. To those who questioned why an eighty-year-old woman would want to have an orgasm, those who suggested the work was not lesbian enough to be at an LGBTIQA+ festival and those who changed their minds about producing the show and would not tell me why – your no to *STARS* made us even more determined to say yes! Your silence made us even more sure that the play raises themes that we all need to talk about. Let's talk!

Lastly and most importantly, *STARS* is dedicated to all us survivors, with pride and power and pleasure forever – enjoy the show!

Mojisola Adebayo, March 2023

For more information about issues relating to Intersex rights or FGM visit https://www.consortium.lgbt/member-directory/intersex-equality-rights-uk/ or https://www.forwarduk.org.uk.

CAST

Mrs and all other characters	Debra Michaels
DJ Son	Bradley Charles

CREATIVE TEAM

Writer	Mojisola Adebayo
Directors	Gail Babb and S. Ama Wray
Designer	Miriam Nabarro
Lighting Designer	Nao Nagai
Animation Artist	Candice Purwin
Music Direction	Debo Adebayo
Creative Captions	Stephen Lloyd
Video Consultant	Gillian Tan
Costume Associate	Maariyah Sharjil
Production Therapist	Dawn Estefan
Community Workshop Facilitators	Sue Mayo and Shanika Warren-Markland
R&D 2018 Director	Rikki Beadle-Blair
R&D 2021 Director	Matthew Xia
R&D Designer	Rajha Shakiry
R&D Intersex Consultant	Valentino Vecchietti
R&D FGM Consultants	FORWARD

PRODUCTION TEAM

Production Manager	James Dawson
Production Manager (cover)	Josephine Tremelling
Company Stage Manager (on the book)	Alison Pottinger
Technical Stage Manager	Stuart Glover
Set Construction	Top Show
Production Photography	Ali Wright
Production Filming	Darius Shu

TAMASHA

Tamasha is a dedicated home for both emerging and established Global Majority artists. A powerhouse of new writing, talent development and digital innovation, we platform and invest in stories that celebrate our rich shared histories and cultures. Proudly both artist and audience driven, we're disrupting, dismantling, and inspiring through bold and imaginative storytelling, providing a place to explore our lived experiences and unique perspectives.

We support theatre makers in gaining the skills, knowledge and creative community to create innovative, new work. Our Developing Artists Programme includes masterclasses, showcases, training programmes and networking opportunities, informed by and responsive to the evolving demands of the creative industries.

We collaborate with partners to commission and produce an artistic programme interweaving live and digital productions, such as audio dramas, walking adventures, magazine-style podcasts and annual touring productions. All staged within and beyond traditional spaces.

Productions over the company's history have included *East Is East* by Ayub Khan Din, *Blood* by Emteaz Hussain, *Approaching Empty* by Ishy Din, *Does My Bomb Look Big in This?* by Nyla Levy, *I Wanna Be Yours* by Zia Ahmed, *10 Nights* by Shahid Iqbal Khan, *Made in India* by Satinder Chohan and *Hakawatis* by Hannah Khalil.

Tamasha.org.uk
Twitter: @TamashaTheatre
Facebook: tamashatheatre
Instagram: tamashatheatre

CEO	Valerie Synmoie
Artistic Director	Pooja Ghai
Lead Producer	Debo Adebayo
Assistant Producer	Samia Djilli
Digital Producer	Tuyet Van Huynh
Administrator	Aitor Gonzalez
Finance Manager	Mandeep Gill
Press Consultant	Nancy Poole
Marketing	Rema Chandran

Board: Deepa Patel (Chair), Shawab Iqbal (Vice Chair), Hannah Miller, Anne Torreggiani, Eileen Bellot, Parmi Makh, Victoria Rudolph

Supported using public funding by
ARTS COUNCIL ENGLAND

INSTITUTE OF CONTEMPORARY ARTS (ICA)

The Institute of Contemporary Arts (ICA) is London's leading space for contemporary culture. We commission, produce and present new work in film, music, performance and the visual arts by today's most progressive artists. In our landmark home on The Mall in central London, we invite artists and audiences to interrogate what it means to live in our world today, with a genre-fluid programme that challenges the past, questions the present and confronts the future. The cross-disciplinary programme encourages these art forms and others to pollinate in new combinations and collaborations. We stage club nights and film festivals, gigs and exhibitions, talks and digital art – with interplay and interaction at the core of all we do. Our history of presenting and promoting visionary new art is unrivalled in London: from Kenneth Anger to Kathy Acker, Kano to Klein, Jackson Pollock to Jean-Michel Basquiat, Gay Sweatshop to Forensic Architecture, Pop Art to queer techno. Today, as ever, our inclusive programme reflects and represents who we are as a disparate and diverse collection of cultures and identities.

Exactly 75 years after a group of artists and poets founded the ICA as an alternative to the mainstream, we are committed more than ever to pave the way for the next generation and to platform creative voices. The ICA continues to celebrate risk and champion innovation, and experimentation across the arts – a playground and a home for today's most vital artists. The ICA is an Arts Council England National Portfolio Organization and supported by the DCMS Culture Recovery Fund.

ica.art/@ICALondon

Director	Bengi Ünsal
Chief Producer	Kiera Blakey
Producer	Natasha Chubbuck
Curator of Talks & Learning	Nisha Eswaran
Head of Communications & Design	Kat Benedict
Marketing & Digital Content Creation Specialist	Jennine Khalik
Ticketing Specialist	Anthony Keigher
Technical Manager	Patrick Brett
Technician	Nicky Drain

GAIL BABB Co-Director

Gail Babb is an award-winning theatre maker who specialises in creating new work that centres and celebrates Black British experiences. As a director and dramaturg, she has created shows for theatres, found sites – including museums, swimming pools and a derelict school – as well as national and international touring. Recent credits include work with Fuel, Brixton House, China Plate, National Youth Theatre, Soho Theatre, Talawa Theatre Company, Coney, Tamasha and Hackney Showroom.

In 2021, she won the Kenneth Tynan Award for Excellence in Dramaturgy and was named one of the Alfred Fagon Awards' 25 Black Champions of Theatre. Gail also facilitates creative processes in community settings and runs the MA in Applied Theatre at Goldsmiths, University of London.

S. AMA WRAY Co-Director

Dr. S. Ama Wray is a performance architect, creator of Embodiology® and Professor of Dance at the University of California, Irvine. For over thirty years she has been performing, directing, choreographing, teaching, researching, speaking and collaborating across three continents. Formerly a performer with London Contemporary Dance Theatre and Rambert Dance Company, she advanced to create JaxxXchange, using the principles of jazz performance to empower communities to embrace and celebrate innovation. Her award-winning creative movement methodology, *Embodiology*®, arose from research into improvisation in West African performance. In 2020, she co-founded AI 4 Afrika, an initiative with choreographers, data scientists, scholars and entrepreneurs to make AI more inclusive and aware of afrikan perspectives. As theatre director, her credits include *Moj of the Antarctic: An African Odyssey* and *Muhammad Ali and Me*, both by Mojisola Adebayo.

MIRIAM NABARRO Designer

Miriam Nabarro is a UK-based scenographer and visual artist. Current projects: *At the Forest's Edge* (RSC), *High Times and Ugly Monsters* (20 Stories High/Graeae) and *Catch* (Clean Break). Previously for Tamasha: *My Name Is...* (Arcola/Tron/UK tour); and with Gail Babbs:

Hatch (Hackney Showrooms/TYPT Talawa). Recent work includes world premieres of *The Bone Sparrow* (Pilot, UK tour), Inua Ellams' *The Little Prince* (Fuel), *Touchy, I Told My Mum I Was Going on an RE Trip*, *Buttercup* (all 20 Stories High/BBC Culture in Quarantine/ Performance Live) as well as award-winning productions of *The Great Game Afghanistan* (Tricycle/US tour), *Dr Korczac's Example* (Royal Exchange/Arcola), *Palace of the End* (Exchange/Traverse/tour), *A Winter's Tale* (Headlong, UK tour). Socially engaged projects include *Processions*, *Sweatbox* and *I Am a Theatre* for Clean Break and projects with Art Refuge UK in Calais.

Miriam is artist in residence at SOAS, University of London. Her printmaking and photographic work is held at the British Library, the Victoria and Albert collection, Bishopsgate Institute, Centre Georges Pompidou, Paris, and in private collections. www.miriamnabarro.co.uk

NAO NAGAI Lighting Designer

Nao Nagai would like to be known a useful passer-by who got curious. However, she is a London-based lighting designer, technical collaborator and performer from Japan. After emigrating to the UK at the age of fifteen, she trained at Rose Bruford College in Lighting Design and has been lighting and collaborating on multi-genre performances internationally. Credits include: *Last Gasp WFH/ Recalibration* (Split Britches), *Dan Daw Show* (Dan Daw Creative Project), *Trouble in Mind* (National Theatre), *Scenes with Girls* (Royal Court), *Yellowman* (Young Vic), *Ceremonial Blue* (Midori Takada and Lafawndah), *Copyright Christmas* (Duckie), *Madama Butterfly, Tosca* (Arcola), *OUT, Night Clubbing* (Rachel Young), *the moment I saw you I knew I could love you* (Curious), *Dr Carnesky's Bleeding Woman* (Marisa Carnesky) and many more. Nao also performs regularly with the cult pop performance group Frank Chickens (winner of Foster's Comedy God Awards). She is a tutor in Lighting Design at Goldsmiths, University of London.

CANDICE PURWIN Animation Artist

Candice Purwin is an illustrator, animator and comics artist based in Edinburgh. Her first graphic novel, *Idle Women: On the Water*, which documented the flagship project by the arts, environment and social justice collaboration of the same, was released in 2020. Recently she has developed the animation for the play *STARS*, and worked closely on illustration projects with Women's Centre Huddersfield, Manchester University Social Studies Department and others. She is currently working on her first fiction graphic novel.

DEBO ADEBAYO Music Direction + DJ Mixes

Debo Adebayo is a theatre and cultural producer, DJ and music publisher. He has worked with companies such as Talawa, Nitro (The Black Theatre Co-operative), Tangle, The Red Room, Utopia Theatre and Collective Artistes. In 2012, he founded music publisher Mix 'n' Sync. He has worked with Tamasha since 2015 and is its Lead Producer. He is also the Deputy Artistic Director (maternity cover) at Paines Plough.

Theatre credits include: *10 Nights* by Shahid Iqbal Khan (2021), *Under the Mask* by Shaan Sahota (2021), *Approaching Empty* by Ishy Din (2019), *Does My Bomb Look Big in This?* by Nyla Levy (2019), *I Wanna Be Yours* by Zia Ahmed (2019) (all for Tamasha as producer), *I Stand Corrected* (producer and music supervisor, Oval House/London, 2012, Artscape/Cape Town, 2012), *Muhammad Ali and Me* (producer and music supervisor, Oval House/London, 2008, Albany/London, 2016), *Moj of the Antarctic* (assistant composer, Oval House/London, 2008, British Council tour of Afrcia, 2008, Lyric Hammersmith/London, 2007). TV: *Invisible* (music supervisor, Random Acts, Channel 4, 2012).

STEPHEN LLOYD Creative Captions

Stephen Lloyd has created captions for companies and venues such as Barbican Centre, Diverse City, Arts Council England, Graeae Theatre Company, Greenwich & Docklands International Festival, Arcola Theatre, Tamasha and many more. He first started to caption his work in 2016, as Artistic Director and founder of gig-theatre company Amplified Theatre, and was the first artist to bring captioned theatre to The Bunker in 2017.

Stephen is currently the Acting Tutor and Project Director at the Royal Academy of Music on their new Junior Academy Musical Theatre course and is an Acting Tutor at the London College of Performing Arts on their BTEC Acting pathway.

An award-winning film and theatre director, he has worked at venues such as Theatre Royal Plymouth, The Bunker, King's Head Theatre, and New Theatre Royal. His indie-musical film *Street Magic* won the award for Best Romantic Short at the Indie X Fest in LA in 2021. As an actor for over ten years, he has played the lead in Graeae's cult musical *Reasons to be Cheerful*, appeared as Boycie in *Rock and Chips* – the BBC prequel to the legendary comedy *Only Fools and Horses* – and in the acclaimed actor-musician production of *Henry V* at the Théâtre National de Nice, France.

GILLIAN TAN Video Consultant

Gillian Tan is a multi-disciplinary designer, working across lighting and video for various theatrical, immersive and interactive experiences. Theatre includes: *South Pacific* (Chichester Festival Theatre/Sadler's Wells/UK tour), *Mind Mangler* (Mischief Theatre/Edinburgh Fringe Festival), *The Apology* (New Earth Theatre), *Bodies* by Ray Young (a sound and performance installation in swimming pools across the UK), *The Body Remembers* (Fuel), *Black Love* (Paines Plough/Belgrade Theatre, Coventry/tiata fahodzi), *Really Big and Really Loud* (Paines Plough/Belgrade Theatre, Coventry), *When the Long Trick's Over* (HighTide), *Cinderella*, *The Awesome Truth* (Polka), *Alyssa*, *Memoirs of a Queen* (Vaudeville), *Aisha and Abhaya* (Royal Ballet/Rambert), *Majestique* (Skråen), *The Song Project – Is in Our Blood* (Royal Court), *4.48 Psychosis* (revival Lyric Hammersmith/Royal Opera House), *La Soirée* (Aldwych Theatre/Southbank Centre/Skråen), *Coraline* (Barbican Theatre/Royal Opera House), *Tamburlaine* (New Earth Theatre/Arcola Theatre), *Invisible Treasure* (Ovalhouse), *Who Do We Think We Are?* (Southwark Playhouse), *Crocodiles* (Royal Exchange, Manchester). Film includes: *NYX and Gazelle Twin Present Deep England*, a performance film by Iain Forsyth and Jane Pollard, and *Held Momentarily* (Royal Academy of Music). She is also a member of the Somerset House Exchange and is the Head of Video at RADA and recently participated in the Unreal Engine Storytelling Fellowship.

MAARIYAH SHARJIL Costume Associate

Maariyah Sharjil is a designer. She is a recent first-class graduate from BA Design for Performance at the Royal Central School of Speech and Drama (2021). Before her design training, Maariyah worked at Sands Films as a costume constructor.

Her most recent productions include: costume researcher for *Life of Pi* (American Repertory Theater), design associate and costume supervisor for *The P-Word* (Bush Theatre), assistant costume supervisor for *The Father and the Assassin* (National Theatre), costume designer for *The Key Workers' Cycle* (Almeida).

DAWN ESTEFAN Production Therapist

Award-winning psychoanalytic psychotherapist Dawn Estefan is a BACP-registered therapist with a clinical expertise in trauma and a special interest in the use of psychoanalytic theory as a way of making sense of our lives and the world we live in. Her unorthodox approach to mental health has seen her collaborate with several organisations, brands and creatives from all art forms over the years solidifying her belief that 'thought and thinking' can also be considered to be a creative process as well as conduit to organisational and personal change.

Dawn is also a writer and social commentator as well as a regular BBC pundit and columnist. She has become an exciting and alternative voice in the therapy world.

Dawn is CEO of Dawn Estefan Creative Thinking and Thought and has a private practice based in north London.

SUE MAYO Community Workshop Facilitator

Sue Mayo is a collaborative theatre maker, working primarily with community and intergenerational groups. She has worked with LIFT, the Royal Court, the Royal Albert Hall and Magic Me, as well as on her own projects, including The Gratitude Enquiry and currently Breaks & Joins; repair as an act of resistance. She is also a researcher and taught at Goldsmiths, University of London, where she was Director of the MA in Applied Theatre until 2022. Her podcast #breaksandjoins is available on all good platforms. www.suemayo.co.uk

SHANIKA WARREN-MARKLAND Community Workshop Facilitator

Shanika Warren-Markland is an actor, writer and creative practitioner. She has worked extensively in the diversity, equity and inclusion sector as well as outreach and creative engagement for a number of organisations including Emergency Exit Arts where she is the Creative Engagement Manager. She also works in the violence against women and girls sector (VAWG) delivering workshops and training on domestic abuse in schools, colleges, universities and businesses across the country, often using creative elements to demonstrate the issue. For Tender, an organisation working to end abuse, she has written a film and an interactive video game for SEND young people regarding issues of healthy relationships and intimate image abuse. She is a keen advocate for diversifying the community arts sector and has worked on many initiatives to bring through global majority facilitators in participatory arts.

DEBRA MICHAELS Mrs and all other characters

Debra Michaels trained at Webber Douglas.

Theatre credits include: Sister Sandrine/Marie in *The Da Vinci Code*, Vernice in *Strange Fruit* (Bush), The Empress in *Aladdin* (Milton Keynes), Maria in *Man of La Mancha*, Mrs Alexander/Various in *The Curious Incident of the Dog in the Night-Time* (National Theatre/UK tour), Manny/Myrtle in *Red Snapper* (Belgrade Theatre), Fairy Godmother in *Cinderella* (Lyric Hammersmith), Sadista in *Sleeping Beauty* (Northcott Theatre), Mama Morton in *Chicago*, The Mother in *Catwalk* (Tricycle), Carmen in *Carmen Jones*, directed by Simon Callow (Old Vic and European tour), *Porgy and Bess*, directed by Trevor Nunn (Glyndebourne and Covent Garden), *Barnum*, *Little Shop of Horrors*, *Soul Train*, *Cinderella*, *Tricksters' Payback*, *Jeckyll and Hyde*, *Four Note Opera*, *A Midsummer Night's Dream* and *The Bottle Imp*.

Television work includes: Mrs Olatunji in *Casualty*, Justine Simpson in *EastEnders*, Headmistress in *Broken*, *Doctors*, *Holby City*, *The Lodge*, *The South Bank Show*, *The Real McCoy* and *Rites*.

Debra has worked as a musical director on *The Wiz* at Riverside Studios and *Singing Bridges* for LWT, and as vocal coach on *Our Own Story* at The Dome. She also co-created and choreographed *The Wedding Dance* which received its premiere at Bolton Octagon prior to a tour.

BRADLEY CHARLES DJ Son

Bradley Charles is a DJ, performer and dancer. Recent credits include *Sylvia* (Old Vic), *In the Willows* (Metta Theatre) and MOVE IT 2022 with Flawless Dance Company. His stage credits also include roles at theatres including the National Theatre, Barbican, Theatre Royal Stratford East, Sadler's Wells, Peacock Theatre and Bristol Old Vic, and with companies including Boy Blue Entertainment, Impact Dance and ZooNation. He was Artistic Director of ZooNation Youth Company from 2019 to 2021 and is currently the company's mentor and wellbeing officer. He was Dance Captain for the London 2012 Olympics Opening Ceremony and Associate Choreographer for *Hex* (National Theatre).

Bradley is a DJ in the UK and internationally, including being resident DJ for Acting Up, Lovers and Friends and UDO Dance Competition, at events for Newham Council including the Mayor's showcase festival (Central Park) and BikeFest (Barking Park), and as part of the 3D Network.

STARS

Dedicated to all us survivors

Characters

Mrs
DJ Son

The female performer who plays **Mrs** *also plays all the other characters except* **DJ Son**, *including:*

GP, **Maryam**, **Chris**, **Church Elders One**, **Two** *and* **Three**,
Saturn, **Pluto**, **Scholars One**, **Two** *and* **Three**, **Mrs's Mum**,
Mrs's Dad, **Terry/Mr**, **Shahana**, **Maxi**, **Dr Money**, **Maxi's
Mum** *and* **Barry**

Pre-show

Music: 'Space is the Place' by Sun Ra. Audience are ideally seated in-the-round or horseshoe to accentuate the storytelling feel. Set not yet fully revealed.

Opening Ritual

A suggested ritual, feel free to experiment: on house clearance there is silence, haze, a mystical, starry feeling. Enter two Black or mixed-heritage performers: one presents as male, the other female. Note: the actors themselves can be of any gender or none but they perform, for now, as male and female. They can also have any kind of body – the production should be inclusive. He is dressed in robes and hat that resonate with the culture of Dogon, Mali, as do all the visual elements of the show. He whirs a bull-roarer over his head, the humming sound represents the voice of the sacred star Sirius B/Po Tolo, signifying the arrival of the Nommo. She represents the Nommo – an African androgynous anthro-amphibian space traveller. She is dressed in costume/headdress/mask inspired by Dogon culture. The two move slowly, ritualistically into the ominous dimly lit space. Arriving centre stage, they turn full circle with the bull-roarer. Whirring subsides and the two performers are still, facing each other. Lights go black and hand-drawn animation of the Nommo story is projected with voice-over and creative captions (artistic surtitles) below. The animation in the play connects in some way all to **Maryam**, *whom we meet later. The animations are* **Maryam***'s drawings; they are what she sees or imagines or even dreams, whether or not we see her in a particular scene. All words spoken in the play are creatively captioned, either embedded into the animations or projected on the set during spoken text, all to support access for people who are D/deaf or hearing impaired (especially as music plays throughout the show). Audio description is also available on headsets and touch-tours can be offered prior to the show for people who are blind or visually impaired. Relaxed performances can also be offered. All efforts should be made to make sure the production is inclusive to all.*

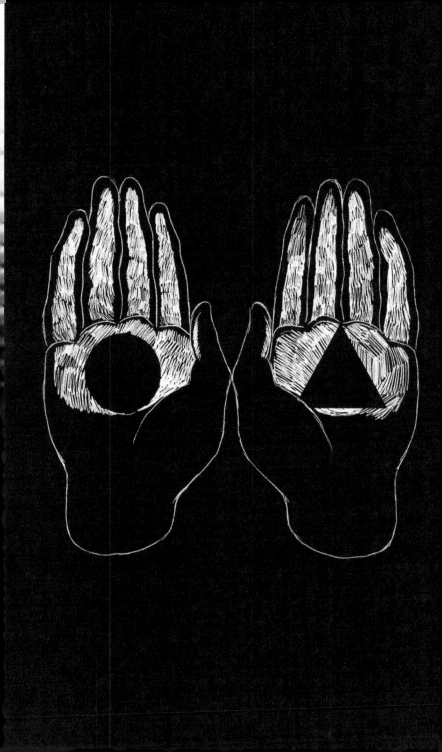

Nommo animation/voice-over:

Both (*calling, slow, in sync*)
Nommo . . . Nommo . . .
Once we were two
When two was one
Space duo, in solo
We Nommo
Both female and male,
Of land and of sea,
From Po Tolo
Comes Nommo
Of Sirius: B.
Beings of twin
Fish-like-body-persons
With feet and fins
Scales and skin
Rainbow chameleons
Ancestral aliens
This is a tale of tails . . .

Scene One: Funeral/New Dawn

*During the animation/voice-over the two performers remove their costumes (used again at the end of the show) in the darkness. At the end of the animation upbeat music (e.g. Hudson Mohawke's 'Scudd Books') kicks in, contrasting the scene. The performers are now revealed as **Mrs**, our protagonist, a Black (or Black mixed-heritage) woman around eighty years old from south-east London, and her son, a DJ in his thirties. **Mrs** and **DJ Son** are dressed for a funeral. **DJ Son** is holding an urn, which he hands to **Mrs**. They embrace, sadly. **Mrs** watches **DJ Son** walking away. He enters his radio studio, raised, upstage left or right. He prepares to play a dance music radio set (mixing live) throughout the show, no pause. Suggestion of the London council-flat kitchen of an elderly lady is revealed. Significant items: fridge, washing machine, radio, kitchen table, perhaps a 1960s lampshade that looks a little like a spaceship hovers, two chairs. However, the set is non-naturalistic. The play is magic in its realism, e.g. all props come from inside the fridge. **Mrs** enters, places the urn on the table, looks at it, a determined look.*

Scene Two: Flash-forward to GP

*A flash-forward in time. 'Scudd Books' cuts out immediately as we find **Mrs** sitting in the chair of the **GP**'s surgery, down centre stage. She faces the audience. 'Peroration Six' by Floating Points plays. Female performer plays **Mrs** and the **GP** (and all characters except **DJ Son**). **Mrs** speaks with a south east London/cockney accent of her time, which is more precise and clipped than the cockney accent of today. Although she is Black, her voice is like any white, Londoner of her time. **GP** is in her thirties, white, English RP. All live spoken text is projected in creative captions, displayed from the DJ's radio studio.*

Mrs   Me husband died

And it's taken my whole life

But doctor,

I've never had one

And I want one

Before I die.

I want to know what it's like.

What is wrong with me?

GP Anorgasmia

Mrs She said.

Ain't that a flower?

GP Also known as 'Coughlan's Syndrome'.

Mrs Nice Irish name.

GP An inability to orgasm. Sometimes because of lack of adequate stimulation, sometimes it's caused by trauma: fight, flight, freeze. Sometimes –

Mrs (*interrupting*) – sometimes, I feel I almost might, when I have a forbidden thought . . . and then I . . . sneeze. Do you think it's connected?

GP I really don't know about that, Mrs . . .

Mrs Could there be a cure?

GP Have you ever tried . . . self-help?

Mrs I had a lavender bath and candles.

GP I mean, perhaps with an electrical device? Not in the bath of course, that would be dangerous. Was there anything else, Mrs . . . We are passed our ten minutes and you are well past menopause so perhaps you'd like to find a hobby instead? And I'd like you to book in for a dementia test – it's just a precaution . . .

Mrs Dementia?

Hobby!

Electrical device?!

I need to find a *cure*.

My orgasm has got to be out there

Somewhere!

Scene Three: Kitchen

Back to the present. **Mrs** *is back in the kitchen looking at the urn on the table as before. There is also a goldfish bowl filled with water (the goldfish is not real), a radio, an ashtray, a packet of cigarettes, a lighter, the* Mirror *newspaper, reading glasses, a half-eaten sandwich and a mug of tea on the table.* **Mrs** *sits. Turns on the radio. Nibbles the sandwich, sips tea, listens to* **DJ Son** *speaking softly, unassuming, through the mic.* **Mrs** *proudly, silently mouths his tag line (below):* 'Taking you through the night, sci-fi style. Frequencies open.'

DJ Son   This is Michael Manners the original AfroCelt on NTX.

Mrs   That's my boy . . .

DJ Son   Show's dedicated to Terry Manners. Taking you through the night, sci-fi style. Frequencies open . . .

DJ Son *plays 'West G Cafeteria' by the Space Dimension Controller.* **Mrs** *listens, takes out a cigarette, clocks it is the last one in the box, lights it, watching the urn.*

Mrs (*quoting* **Mr**, *her dead husband*)   'What now, Mrs?' What now . . . (*Music underscores.* **Mrs** *sits, takes her reading glasses, opens the newspaper and reads her horoscope.*) 'Planetary activity in Leo, and today's new moon marks the start of a personal adventure – even at the onset of winter. Despite the fact a pursuit of yours turned out to be a flight of fancy, you should accept an invitation from afar, without hesitation. Keep doors open. Breathe new air. Throw caution to the wind.'

(*To the fish in the goldfish bowl.*) Well, Cat, what do we make of that?

Mrs *listens in her mind to Cat, the fish, who she hears saying 'time to give up smoking'. Cat's text is also captioned and there could be fish animation here.*

Agreed.

Mrs *draws deep on her last cigarette. Stubs it out. Takes a deep breath, she might cough. Sips tea. Pauses at a newspaper article.*

'Government plans to send refugees into space.

First came Brexit, now – Spexit: Space exit'

(*Imagining.*) Immigrants on Mars . . .

Asylum on Saturn . . .

Aliens meet the aliens . . .

(*Reading an advert next to the article.*) 'Whether you are a migrant, exile or adventurous expat, you can apply for Project Spexit in partnership with the Virgin Space Travel Programme. Budget planet relocation (one way) or luxury space holiday (return). Terms and conditions . . . apply online now!'

Wow.

'www.' . . .

Disappointed as she is not online.

Don't no one use pen and paper anymore . . .

DJ Son   This is Space Dimension Controller with 'West G Cafeteria'.

Mrs   Cat food! How rude, I am forgetting myself.

She gets fish food from the fridge which stores all props, empties the container of fish flakes – only a few are left, feels guilty for neglecting 'Cat'.

Whatchu lookin at me like that for? Shop's shut. You'll have to wait 'til morning . . . (**Mrs** *hears 'Cat' suggesting, 'How about a sprinkling of the old man?' The fish's lines are also captioned.* **Mrs** *reacts shocked.*) I can't do that!

She hears 'Cat' saying, 'Well, he ate fish didn't he?'

You're not wrong about that, Cat.

Mr probably polished off several of your relatives,

Beer battered with vinegar and chips,

Licking his lips,

Pissed.

She picks up the urn, impersonating **Mr**. *Here and throughout, the performer embodies the action described, acts out the memories, keep it live.*

Staggering back to manhandle his Mrs every Friday,
Saturday, any day, any night

So –

DJ Son *and* **Mrs** (*simultaneously without awareness of each other*)
– what goes around . . .

DJ Son   comes around.

Music. **Mrs** *empties the ashes from the urn into the goldfish bowl. The fish gobbles the ashes.* **Mrs** *laughs.*

DJ Son   'Fight'. This track is one of mine on Native City.
Memories of my old man, Terry.

Mrs *hears her son, shame. Then to the audience, her confessors.*

Mrs   What must you think of me?

(*Justifying herself.*) Sixty years of 'honour and obey'

I was a zombie, a slave,

The *living* dead, that was me.

He don't feel nothing now do he?

He don't feel nothing at all.

So nothing's changed there.

There's not a husband, a father

Only a jailer.

But I've served my time in this space.

I've known my place.

She starts saying the line along with the music, enjoying the freedom.

Yeah I've served my time in this space,

I've known my place.

What *now*?

DJ Son   'Travlin' by Norm Talley . . .

Sound of doorbell. Animation projected: through a spyhole, on the landing of the council block, we see a girl, around eleven years old, of African descent, ringing the doorbell, desperate to use the toilet and **Mrs** *letting her in. Animation could become abstract to convey time passing, the moon (symbolising* **Mrs**'s *husband) disappears. The sun (symbolising the girl) rises. Quick change into* **Mrs**'s *comfy indoor clothes.*

Scene Four: Mrs and Maryam Become Friends

Another doorbell. **Mrs** *is brighter, comfy clothes, slippers, now smoking a vape. The girl (***Maryam***) is at the door.* **Maryam** *is polite, confident, innocent, matter-of-fact; she speaks RP English but as a second language, perhaps the faintest memory of somewhere in Africa.*

Mrs   Hello again, little friend.

Maryam   I brought you chocolates, for my birthday. (*Hands a box of Celebrations chocolates.*)

Mrs   It's not my birthday.

Maryam   I know, that's why I said it, *my* birthday.

Mrs   Oh, happy birthday. Aren't you the one supposed to be getting presents?

Maryam   I got lots of presents. I got . . . holiday.

Mrs   Oh . . . going anywhere nice?

Maryam   Been already. Came back for big school starting. Was saving Celebrations but Mum said I should give them to you to say thank you.

Mrs   What for?

Maryam   Yesterday's toilet.

Mrs   Oh right. No need to thank me, just being neighbourly but . . . come in and have a Celebration anyway.

They go inside. **Mrs** *goes over to the table with* **Maryam***, who is scared of the fish.*

Mrs   Make yourself at home. He's all right, he don't bite. If my furry friend Feena was still alive she'd likely have a scratch but this Cat's safe in his bowl.

Maryam *looks confused.* **Mrs** *empties a few of the chocolates on the table.*

Mrs (*referring to the chocolates*)   What's your favourite?

Maryam   Number 3: Galaxy. Number 2: Milky Way. Number 1: Mars. I love planets and stars.

Mrs   You wanna apply for that Spexit.

Maryam   Doing a project for school. And when I grow up I am going be a spacewoman.

Mrs   Oooh a little Lieutenant Uhura. I always felt a bit like her when I worked at British Telecom. (*Like Uhura.*) 'Hailing frequencies open, Captain.'

Maryam   What?

Mrs   *Star Trek*.

Maryam   No, *Star Trek* is not real. I am going to be real, like Mae Jemison.

Mrs   Who?

Maryam   First Black woman up there. But I will be first from my country. (*She points up.*)

Mrs (*like E.T.*)   'Phone home' . . .

Maryam   Huh?

Mrs   *E.T.*

Maryam   I don't know what you are talking about.

Mrs (*like Tom Hanks in* Apollo 13)   'Houston, we have a problem.'

Maryam   I know. I need more science.

Mrs   You better have a Mars then. I'll put the kettle on.

(*To the audience.*) And that's how it started.

We finished off the Celebrations

Every afternoon after school

While she worked on her stars project.

Then she'd have a pee and I'd a vape and a cup of tea.

Short animation as **Mrs** *picks up* **Maryam**'s *stars project book and flicks through the pages. We briefly see fragments of* **Maryam**'s *drawings, writing, diagrams . . .*

Mrs   'What are you doing in there, Mary . . .?'

She said she liked the quiet,

She says she liked my toilet,

The woolly loo-roll holder – she reads astronomy.

Feeling sorry for the grieving old lady

She'd fetch me the *Mirror*, daily.

Maryam   But *Metro* is free?

Mrs   Sometimes you gotta pay for quality, Mary.

Her name ain't even Mary,

Her name is Maryam

But no one at school can say it right

And Mary sounds less Muslim.

She went to Catholic school see,

The primary attached to my parish

And since that soldier got his head chopped off in Woolwich

It is easier to be a Mary than a Maryam.

She says the rosary several times throughout the play.

> Hail Mary, full of grace
> The Lord is with thee
> Blessed art thee amongst women
> And blessed is the fruit of thy womb, Jesus

DJ Son   Here's Rhythm Is Rhythm with 'Strings of Life' . . .

Scene Five: Memories of Church and Children

Mrs   I got born again for ten minutes

Searching for 'the final frontier'

When Mr was having his affair with Venus

(*Calling towards flat in the opposite block.*) from over there!

I was lonely and they give you free chicken on a Sunday.

But Venus eventually had enough of his drinking n' pissing
in the bed so he came back and shat in ours instead

And I went back to mass.

I dunno,

Maybe I needed to believe leaving him was a sin,

Maybe I'm scared of it:

Freedom.

And being Catholic is much more straightforward than
being a happy-clappy,

All those dancing socks-in-sandals –

You know where you stand when you're in Rome

*She re-plays her time in a born-again, mainly white, Evangelical
Christian church. Goes into the audience.*

I could just never fall in the

Evangelical hall,

I've never been very good at being ecstatic.

I look around one revival

And it's like they're all having seizures,

Trembling, heaving and talking in tongues:

'MymamamasgottaSuzukimypapasgottaHondamypapas
gottaSuzukimymamasgottaHondaaaaaiwannaHyundai
wannaHyundaiwannaHyundai . . .'

But I don't go nowhere

I'm just stood there

And no matter how hard the preacher push-push-pushes
(*attempting to 'slay' someone 'in-the-spirit', she reaches towards a
carefully chosen audience member*) my head

I just can't let go of my bones.

Returning to the stage/on the bus.

When it's all over I have chips and curry sauce on the bus
back to Woolwich.

My kind of communion.

Chris always waits for me to leave the service

Pretends he's going the same way,

He's one of those hippy holys . . .

Chris   Jesus got me off heroin – hallelujah.

Mrs   Praise the Lord.

Church was full of unhappy wives and people with addictions,

Chris gets me talking on the bus about unlikely attractions

How he likes –

Chris   older women and there's nothing against it in the Bible, Old Testament or New . . .

Mrs   And as I dunked my chips in the curry sauce I confessed to him that I – sometimes feel drawn to women and my husband's my biggest regret.

He went silent.

I hadn't a clue it was me Chris had a crush on.

Not very Christ-like

I was fucking forty-four, he could have been my son!

(*Wistful.*) But my son hadn't yet come

I imagined him to be waiting on a star . . .

And when by some miracle at forty-six I managed to hatch one good egg (*picking up the radio*)

And my little boy finally arrived! (*Clutching the radio to her chest.*)

And I squeeeeeeeze him close to my breast for eighteen years until he says –

DJ Son (*suffocated*)   I can't bear it anymore, Mum.

Mrs   And he leaves me.

To study music at uni and then spinning his discs around the world . . . (*Quoting Spock, as if saying goodbye.*) 'Live long and prosper', son.

He's got his own radio show now. (*She pauses to listen then speaks into the radio as if her son is tiny.*) Done all right for yourself haven't you, my little Mikey . . .

DJ Son   No one calls me 'Mikey', Mum. (*Quoting his business card.*) Michael Manners: Music Producer. DJ. Broadcaster.

Mrs   And I think –

(*Sudden rage, directed at her son.*) Weren't it me that ripped

To arsehole from fanny squeezing your big head out of me

Then clawed my way through the menopause with you screeeeeaming at me?

Weren't it me that worked day *and* night shifts all them years to put music in your fingers and ears?

Weren't it me that stood in the way of you and Mr's fist

So you wouldn't know what you had missed?

– I can call you what I like, you arrogant little shit!

And then I caught my thought.

Mother Mary forgive me.

'Yes of course: Michael.

Cuppa tea?

Where's my manners?

I forget.'

Yeah, he's done all right for himself Michael, considering . . .

Where was I? –

DJ Son   'Lunar' . . . track's by Acre.

Mrs   Back to the bus with Chris

Who's half the man my son's grown up to be.

Prick goes and tells someone giving him 'spiritual counselling'

That he's got an obsession for some kind of . . . (*whisper*) lesbian.

'Course it goes around the congregation like a bush fire.

They haul me in to an 'emergency house meeting' (*acting out the memory*)

I have to take a shift off

Semi-detached in Greenwich

Ornate iron gate, original tiling,

I think to myself, now that's a lot of tithing.

They sit me down at the big oak kitchen table,

And without so much as a 'howdy-do' or a 'Hallelu'

Pull down the Velux (*pronounced 'veloo'*) blinds announcing –

Playing **Church Elders**.

Church Elder One   Your body is a temple and you haven't kept it clean.

Church Elder Two   That is why your husband treats you –

Mrs   the way he did.

Church Elder Three   That's why he turns to other women and drink.

Mrs   The born-agains said –

Church Elder One   Your womb has an omen, Satan has a hold.

Church Elder Two   That is why you cannot conceive.

Church Elder Three   Believe-believe-believe.

Mrs   And they try to squeeze the

Church Elder One   deeemon of lesbianism out-out-out!

Mrs   of me. Declaring it –

Church Elder One   entered in through horoscopes,

Church Elder Two   sci-fi films

Church Elder Three   and pagans in your *African* ancestry.

Mrs   Out comes a saucepan (*re-playing with the goldfish bowl*)

'Le Creuset' (*pronounced 'le-cru-zay'*) no less

A big heavy orange one

Very middle class

All place their white hands on my Black head, shoulders, breasts

And press-press-press

And there's me, leaning over the saucepan,

And there's them, expecting the

Church Elder One   EVIL SPIRIT

Mrs   to come out in my vomit

But all I can manage is a little bit of spit.

(*Ironic.*) Such a disappointment. (*Returns the goldfish bowl.*)

Never felt quite right with the Evangelicals after that.

And then when Mr finally pulls his penis out of Venus

And they all go

Church Elder One   Praise be! Our prayers have been answered.

Mrs   And I get pregnant with my son and the elders call another house meeting

Church Elder Two   Just in case there's another demon.

Mrs   And then that Freddie Mercury from Queen dies

And the leader stands up in the Sunday celebration and says

Church Elder One   Mercury got what he deserved, AIDS, the curse –

Mrs   I says no.

Enough!

None of this sounds like gentle Jesus or Mother Mary to me

And I love 'Bohemian Rhapsody',

Now Freddie could take you to outer space . . .

'Bohemian Rhapsody' mixes in momentarily with animation from **Maryam**'s *stars book.* **Mrs** *flicks through the book, enjoying the music.*

Scene Six: Mrs and Maryam Observe the Neighbours

Mrs *and* **Maryam** *watch the neighbours from the window.* **DJ Son** *mixes in 'Moon Dance'.*

Mrs   Mary changed my night today.

This flat is the deck of the Starship Enterprise.

(*Quoting* Star Trek.) 'It's life', Maryam, 'but not as we know it.'

DJ Son   'Moon Dance' on Tribe.

Mrs   We're watching the whole constellation of the council estate.

We survey 'neighbour planets' over kitchen plates.

Animation of planets/people described below.

She talks me through it all while I have a vape.

Maryam   The universe accelerates.

Mrs   But looks like our estate is going backwards . . . Look at him, on his phone by the railing, raging (*impersonating the young blood from the estate*), 'It's the system, it's the system' . . .

A game, naming the neighbours after planets:

Maryam   Jupiter. Hothead. Full of gas. Could have been a star . . . Look, Neptune is going out. Only after sunset you see him . . . dark rings around his eyes.

Mrs   Probably working shifts. And look who's coming across the playground.

Maryam   Saturn.

Mrs   Stunning.

Maryam   Big rings in her ears.

Mrs   Afro-centric Empress, (**Mrs** *calls*) yes my sister! Saturn!

Saturn   Greetings, Auntie!

Mrs   *Auntie? (She is disappointed, realising how old she appears.)*

Maryam   Look, sitting on the bench, Uranus!

Mrs   Don't be rude.

Maryam   Mrs, your jokes are older than you. Uranus looks like his face flipped over. And see, Pluto coming home with her shopping. Pluto's not a real planet. She's a dwarf.

Mrs   Don't call her that. She's your height and you wouldn't like it. Gets laughed at but gets on with it. (*Calls out to the woman of short stature passing, with her thumb up.*) Respect! (*The woman looks up.*)

Pluto (*a little cynically*)   Hi.

Mrs   And look who it ain't. (*Kisses her teeth.*)

Maryam   Venus? She is really hot. (**Mrs** *grunts.*) And he is really cold, my favourite.

Mrs   Where?

Maryam   The homeless man in big winter coat and bright red face. All year round.

Mrs *sings a section from David Bowie's 'Life on Mars'.*

Maryam *is laughing and applauding.*

Mrs (*to the radio*)   Let's have a bit of Bowie, Mikey!

Those were the days. Just never thought I'd outlive him.

Maryam   Your husband?

Mrs   No. David Bowie! South London's finest.

Maryam   Stormzy is much better!

Mrs (*like Stormzy*)   'You're getting way too big for your boots.'

They laugh.

No . . . I always knew I'd outlive Mr. He was weak.

Maryam   But he loved you?

Mrs   He might have done. He just didn't know how. Love is what you do, innit?

DJ Son   I'm playing this one on a promise. Here's 'Falling Rizlas' from Actress . . .

They listen to the gentle music for a moment.

Mrs   Who am I then?

Maryam   Earth.

Mrs   Me? Planet Earth? No.

Maryam   Yes. You are.

Mrs   Why?

Maryam   Because, you are mostly blue and covered in clouds.

Mrs   Oh.

Maryam   And Mr, he is like the moon, always following you around, even though he is dead.

Mrs   Blimey.

Maryam   And Mrs you are not a healthy planet (*pointing to the vape*). This is not good for you. I read it in *Metro*.

Mrs   Heavens. (*Slightly aggressive.*) Anything else, Dr Spock?

Maryam (*a joke*)   Dr *who*?

Mrs   Ha! (*Conceding defeat to Mary.*) You win. (*Puts her vape away, in the fridge.*)

(*Sadly admitting.*) I'm not exactly . . . 'Mother' Earth then.

Maryam   Sorry. (*I.e. no you're not 'Mother' Earth.*)

Mrs   It's all right. You're probably right. But you little one are the sun, brightening up my day.

A sad pause.

Maryam (*sadly, disclosing*)   If I am the sun

Maybe that is why

I burn.

If I am the sun,

Maybe that is why

If you looked at me

You would close your eyes . . .

Perhaps I will build a rocket

For my school project

So I can fly closer

To myself

And then I will keep on flying, *way up*

(*Line sung like acoustic version of Jamila Woods' song 'Way Up'.*)

After myself

To a little star in the dark

'Po Tolo'/Home

From where the 'Nommos' come . . .

DJ Son   'Bouramsy' from Lil Silva.

Nommo Story Part One: Animation Interlude

Animation. **Maryam** *is recounting the story of the Nommo to* **Mrs***, while she is drawing them for her stars school project. We see the drawings. Text in voice-over/subtitles.*

Mrs   So, the story goes . . .

Maryam   The Nommos

Were migrants from across the cosmos

Sailing the sky to planet Earth.

Descendants from a star that you and I cannot see –

Mrs   With naked eyes at least –

Maryam   Sirius B.

And for thousands of years,

Sirius A we could see

But Sirius B was known only

To the Dogon of Mali.

Mrs   Cousins to the Pharoahs?

Maryam   Who knows.

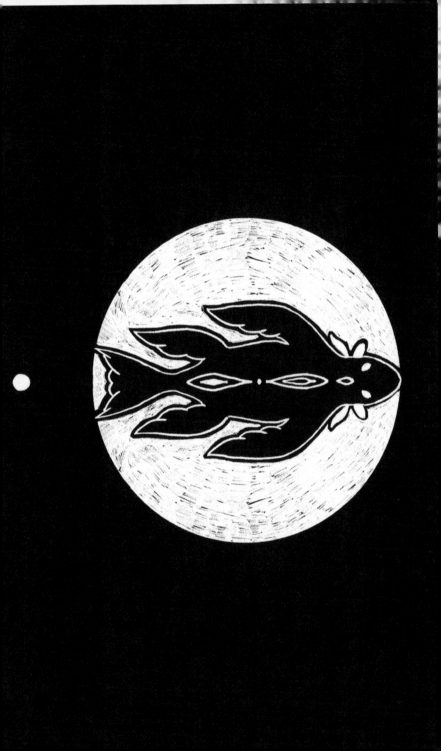

The Dogon call Sirius B 'Po Tolo'.

'Po'?

Mrs   – star?

Maryam   Tolo – the tiniest white seed you can scatter in a field . . .

The white scientists could not see this star.

Mrs   Nor could the Dogon, it's too small, too far.

Maryam   But their fathers were told of Po Tolo

By?

Mrs   – the Nimmos!

Maryam (*correcting* **Mrs**)   The *Nommos*!

Ancestor aliens sailing to Africa in a spaceship from Sirius B.

Mrs   Seriously?

Maryam   They say Sirius B orbits Sirius A every half of a century . . .

And Dogon paint all they know of the cosmos from the Nommos

On the walls of houses,

Celebrating with rituals, sculptures, dances!

Dogon art exhibits in New York–London–Paris

Mrs   Making Picasso a modernist and careers for anthropologists.

Maryam   And then one day

Through a big telescope

Mrs   Old blue eyes said

(*Impersonating an English scholar.*) 'Indeed

Sirius has a B that cannot – *nakedly* – be seen'

And he took a photo,

Maryam   In 1970.

Mrs   European scholars –

Mrs *as the* **Scholars**.

Scholar One   What a wonder!

The star really is very, very, dense

Just as that remote tribe said

And it is as white as snow . . .

But how could these old Black Africans know?

Scholar Two   Their cave paintings reveal the vastness of the universe!

Before *us* they knew of Jupiter's moons!

And the rings of Saturn – they could see!

And Sirius B *does* orbit Sirius A every fifty years *precisely*.

Scholar Three   They knew that the planets revolve around the sun

And that the earth was born from a big *big* bang.

While we were still drawing maps of the earth as flat

And believed the horizon was the end of it.

When we were still too scared to set sail,

For fear our boats would fall off into hell,

When we still believed the sun revolved around *us*

Scholar Two   And the dark creatures of the earth were wicked primitive savages.

Scholar One   While we were burning witches and heretics

Mrs   It seems these Africans were intergalactic!

Maryam   The Dogon knew all about Sirius

Mrs   How could that be? . . .

Maryam   We told you! We were told by? . . .

Mrs (*getting it right this time*)   the Nommos!

Extraterrestrial Afro-hermaphrodite anthro-amphibian migrants!

Maryam   Both male and

Mrs   female.

Maryam   Of land and

Mrs   of sea.

Maryam   Like humans and

Mrs   fish!

Maryam   With feet and

Mrs   fins!

Maryam   Scales and

Mrs   skin.

Maryam   Ancestor aliens!

Rainbow chameleons!

Mrs   This is a tale of tails . . .

DJ Son   Toumani Diabate: 'Salaman'.

Scene Seven: Maryam's Revelation

Mrs   She said

Maryam   it burnt

Mrs   Like no temperature you could touch,

When she was cut,

In the summer holidays.

Her eyes clenched shut.

Hands pressing her head, shoulders, legs . . .

Maryam   It was so painful.

Mrs   Shameful.

But she insisted –

Maryam   they did it because they love me.

Mrs   Her parents.

That's why she wouldn't – (*grabbing her mobile phone*)

'Let me phone the police! I should call social services!'

Maryam   No! Please, Mrs, don't say, they might take me away . . .

Mrs   And I know its selfish but

I was afraid they might take her from me too . . .

So 'it's our little secret'.

Why she liked to use my toilet.

Why it took her fifteen minutes to pee.

Why it –

Maryam (*through pain*)   stings.

Mrs   And she transports herself –

Maryam   to the stars!

A monologue from **Maryam**, *sitting on the toilet, clutching a book called* Stars *by Andrew King, reciting what she has learnt to distract herself from excruciating pain.*

Maryam   'Every atom of your body

Was once part of a star.'

Part of a star . . .

Part of a star . . .

An atom is smallest matter

That cannot be cut.[1]

Cannot be cut.

Can never be cut

To the stars you must return,

Maryam,

To the stars you must return . . .

Mrs So that was why she shuffled her feet across the estate

Why she wouldn't drink

Why she was losing weight

No matter how many Galaxys she ate.

She said (*recovering from the pain momentarily*).

Maryam When you look into the stars you look into the past . . .

But you can't change it.

Mrs If I could,

I would . . .

DJ Son *rewinds the track and plays forward again with 'Bouramsy' over Nommo animation interlude two.*

Nommo Story Part Two: Animation Interlude

Text is in voice-over/captions as with part one.

Maryam But,

---

1 Paraphrased from Andrew King's *Stars: A Very Short Introduction* (Oxford: Oxford University Press, 2012), pp. 1 and 29.

Just like Earth and moon are partners in destiny

Just like Sirius B is one part only of a shining binary

With Sirius A –

Mrs   The Dog Star – man's brightest friend

This starry story also has a companion:

Maryam   The Dogon *also* believe in one God,

In the sky

Mrs   sounds familiar

Maryam   Amma,

Who wanted the Earth as His celestial . . . (*Hesitating, shy of the subject.*)

Mrs   (sexual) partner

Maryam   But he could not . . . (*Hesitating.*)

Mrs   'mount her'

Maryam   Because her . . . (*Hesitating.*)

Mrs   'mountain' was too big

(*Aside just for the adult audience.*) It got in the way, he couldn't get it in.

Maryam   The wilful single mother Earth gave birth

To a jackal, a devil instead!

Mrs   Whom Amma rejects as he could not possibly be the father.

Maryam   The devil/jackal runs around bringing the world into disorder.

So Amma created the Nommo as messengers, saviours of the world!

But even though the Nommo are

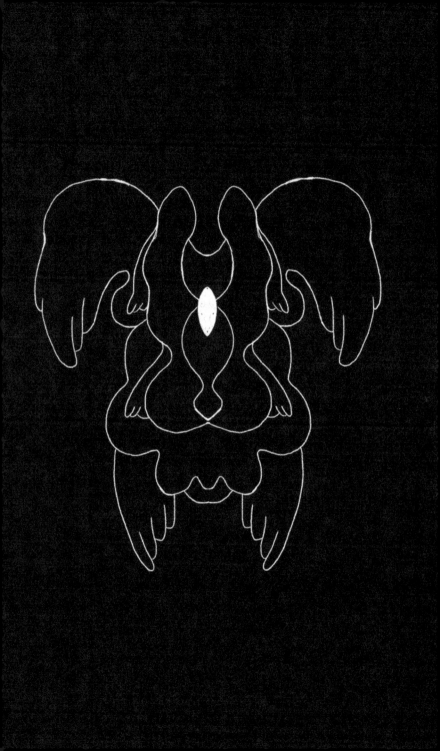

Mrs   transmitters of all the Dogon know,

Maryam   To the people, Nommo look . . . (*Hesitating.*)

Mrs   troubling,

As doubling androgynes,

Their bodies ugly and fishy with excessively fleshy
differing . . .

Maryam   So Dogon believe to stop the world from all this
disorder

Mrs   Brought to the world by the reckless devil-jackal son
of un-mountable mother,

Maryam   A boy must be made to look like a boy and a girl
must be made to look like a girl and we must look like
Nommo –

Mrs   – no more!

A duel of duals has ensued since then

Repeated the world over

In religions, traditions, medicine.

Justified

With knives,

Scalpels, razor blades and needles in hand

To make a woman a woman

Maryam   and a man no less than a man . . .

Mrs   This is an old tale of tails . . .

Maryam   But, once we were two

Mrs   When two was one

Maryam   And some of us want to go home.

End animation.

DJ Son   – Here's 'Bright Star', the Sunset Remix.

Track plays.

Scene Eight: Why?

Mrs   Why? . . .

Maryam   Tradition.

Mrs   Yes but why?

Tradition.

Later she said:

Maryam   Mrs, I asked my mum, about that thing.

Mrs   Did you? What did she say?

Maryam   She said English people don't understand and I should never talk about it. I'm not talking about it, OK, Mrs?

Mrs   OK.

Maryam   She said it happened to my brother too, when he was thirteen, but I was younger and braver. I got bigger party, I got new dress and Elsa dolly from *Frozen* you know 'let it go, let it go . . .' OK, I am too old but still everybody happy, everybody give us money – much more than my brother!

Mrs   That's different, Mary, what they cut off the boys ain't the same.

Maryam   It's not true. My mum said, little girls have a bit, little boys have a bit, both gets cut, because if we didn't, boys grow into girls and girls grow into boys and no one knows who is who.

Mrs   It don't grow into a willy, Mary . . .

Maryam   (*upset*)   And then I ask why they chose me, why I cannot pee why it hurt so much, Mum? . . . (*Recovering.*) She says it happen to her too, and to my grandmother and to every lady body I know in my family since the beginning of time. She says it make us clean and calm. Pure and perfect girl for marriage.

Mrs   Mary, it's not right.

Maryam   But my mum said!

Mrs   Mary, what you got, what you *had*, down there, no one is supposed to touch unless you want them to, and when they do it's supposed to feel . . . (*She isn't sure how it's supposed to feel.*)

Maryam   It's supposed to feel? . . .

Mrs   Nice.

Maryam   Nice? (*I.e. is that all?*)

Mrs (*realising the inadequacy of 'nice'*)   Like the best thing in the whole world!

Maryam   What is the best thing in the whole world?

Mrs   I dunno. Ice cream. It's supposed to feel like ice cream in the summer down there. It won't make much difference to your brother, Mary, except he'll probably never get his winkle caught in his zipper.

Maryam   I don't understand.

Mrs   Neither do I.

Maryam   It is supposed to feel nice? It just *hurts* . . .

Pause.

You feel nice? With Mr?

Mrs   You can't ask me that!

Maryam   Why you ask me questions then?! I am not a girl any more Mrs. I know things now.

Mrs   I don't feel nothing, he's dead.

Maryam   No, before he went to heaven? . . . What was it like, on your wedding night?

Mrs   He's not in heaven, Mary, there's not a hell big enough for him and it was never like ice cream. I only married him because I thought I had to after what happened in the fridge.

Maryam   Fridge?

Mrs   This ain't about me, Maryam. You and me, dear, it is not the same.

Maryam   Why?

Mrs   Because you're just a child and I'm an old girl. I'm a soft old bourbon in the bottom of the biscuit tin. I've had my chance at happiness, you ain't!

Maryam (*defensive, angry*)   I have happy chances, lots of them. You are making me sad! I am going be a spacewoman. Like Nommo! My mum and dad love me. They're not like you and Mr! This our culture. If I didn't get cut no husband would want me. And what will happen to me if no one will want me in this far away country where no one says hello, how is your mother, father, sister, brother? . . . My family love me . . . It's just . . . (*Terrible pain.*) Owwwwwwww . . . I have to pee.

Mrs   She shoved past me and then left straight after that. (*She gets her vape. Smokes a little.*) Didn't stop for chocolate or a chat. Came back the next day but wouldn't cross my doorstep. Holds that doll from *Frozen* in a shiny green dress. Thrust it in my face –

Maryam (*with doll*)   Look!

Mrs   'Let it go, let it go . . .' You coming in?

Maryam   Underneath – LOOK!

Mrs   What is it?

Maryam   Nothing. Nothing there. Just like me. I am pretty.

Mrs   You are pretty, Mary.

You need to pee? Come inside –

Maryam   – NO! Mum says (*recalling her mother*), 'Maryam, come. Why only *you* goes to her house? Hm? You know people in this country always doing funny funny things to children. I see it on TV every day. Maybe she is a paedo. Maybe she is a witch. Stay away from that old woman. OK? Come here. (*Cuddles her daughter/self.*) Good girl.'

Maybe I am cut but you are cut too, Mrs. Cut off and covered in scars. But I am going to the stars. I am being a spacewoman, the first woman from my country and I don't need this dirty thing. My mother and my father they brought me here, they (*quoting her father*) 'sacrificed everything and provide everything'. I don't need anything. And when I grow up I will provide them.

Mrs   That's right. That's right. Look come inside and let's –

Maryam   No, no, no! There is nothing for me inside. There is nothing for you! Just a cigarette that is not a cigarette, a cat that is really a fish, science that is fiction, the *Mirror* with no reflection – just made-up stars and a son who hides inside the radio to keep away from YOU! Sorry. Sorry. You should go outside, Mrs, instead of watching it from the window. Mum says I am not allowed to come anymore.

Mrs   And she starts to cry and she starts to pee and she shuffles away, across the estate.

What about your school project? Mary! Maryam! Your book! (*Waving the stars school project book which has been left behind.*)

She didn't look back.

I watched out from my window, all half term, but I didn't see her. So I done like she said. I go outside (*acting out the memory*), knock on their door. (*Pause.*) Nothing. Look through the letter box and . . . a black hole . . . Like they were never there. And ever since that night, I been having this recurring dream . . .

DJ Son   '3am' . . . from Bearcubs . . .

Scene Nine: Eclipse

Animation of the dream, with music and **DJ Son**'s *voice-over/ captions.*

DJ Son (*voiceover*)   The cold moon passes in front of the sun.

We all stand in the playground with cardboard glasses on.

All the neighbours look up at the sky,

But you are looking at the neighbours,

Searching the crowd, for her.

Some cry, some cheer, some shiver with fear.

The birds fall silent,

And we all feel bitterly cold.

It starts to rain

And when we go back up to the flat,

The door is open,

The radio is white noise,

And the fish is floating in the bowl . . .

And you know . . .

You *know* . . .

(*Quoting the film* Blade Runner:) All those moments will be lost in time.

Like tears in rain.

Time to die . . .

End animation/voiceover.

Maryam   Gravity is a grave,

Mrs   she'd say . . .

Maryam   It can only go one way . . . No matter how hard we pray . . .

Scene Ten: Call Michael

Mrs (*distressed*)   I couldn't go back to mass after that. I had no stomach for praying to a virgin. I had no stomach for tradition, religion. I had no stomach for any of it. I want to leave this flat, this planet. (**Mrs** *gets her phone, music shifts, 'Elegant, and Never Tiring' by Lorenzo Senny.*) I phone my Mikey in the middle of the night, crying, 'I've had enough, "beam me up", I wanna go to the stars, with Mary.' He thought I meant that euthanasia clinic in Switzerland. (*Crying, distraught.*) 'No, no you don't understand, Mary came to me, Mary revealed it all, and she made me think about everything I've denied in my life and then she just disappeared as if she was never there, as if she was just a story in the *Mirror* and then last night I had a dream about an eclipse and I heard your voice and now I think she might be dead and she was my sun, my son, she was my reason for getting up in the morning. Michael, Michael, *listen*: at the centre of the whole constellation, there's a bright little girl, there's no future without her but no one can stand to face her . . . We close our eyes. This is your mother, 'signing off, signing off . . .' (*Beat. Recovers composure.*) That brought him home for Christmas. (**DJ Son** *comes down from his studio, sits with his mum.*) Got cover for his radio show and bought me (*unwraps the gift from* **DJ Son**, *delighted*) an 'iPad'! Spends Boxing Day teaching me how to use it.

DJ Son   You can look up your stars. Even does crosswords.

Mrs   Ohhh . . . And do you think I can send one of them 'emails' on this?

DJ Son   It's a whole universe in there, Mum.

Mrs   Our first Mr-less Christmas. Watched old clips from *Star Trek*!

Now I can apply for that Spexit. (*Quoting her horoscope.*) 'The start of a personal adventure.' That's what my stars said.

DJ Son   Live long and prosper, Mum.

DJ Son *returns to his radio studio.*

Mrs   Mary will be up there! Betcha!

DJ Son   That was 'Elegant, and Never Tiring' by Lorenzo Senni . . . Time to 'Chase the Devil' with The Upsetters . . . and Max Romeo.

Scene Eleven: Mrs's Biography

Mrs *speaks during the opening dub section of the track. She searches on her iPad.*

Mrs   Project Spexit/Virgin Space Travel Programme. Application. (*Like Richard Branson.*) 'So, first off, tell us a bit about yourself . . .'

Listens to music, rocking, smoking her vape, thinking about what to write on the application. She speaks after the opening lyrics. The track switches to dub version.

Mrs   During the war I was born, 1944

Throwaway baby of a runaway English wife and a Black American GI

But a Bajan mum and Irish dad rescue me

From a children's home.

Black and white Catholics doing the Lambeth Walk

Mum and Dad were the talk of Southwark.

They always wanted a baby

And didn't mind the controversy.

I was three when they got me

And me mum said I was frozen,

Staring off into space

Whatever they did to me in that place it was no home.

But eventually I learnt to look at adults again

Dreamt of becoming our school's first brown nun,

I could never imagine growing up to marry a man

And that was all that was expected of you back then.

I loved needlework and I was good at Latin,

Weren't I qualified?

But Mum said –

Mrs's Mum (*Bajan, gentle*)   Why on earth you want to be a nun – be a nurse like me, that's close enough.

But Dad said –

Mrs's Dad (*Irish, soft*)   Sure we need money coming in if we we're ever gonna build that house in Saint Lucy.

Mrs   So just before I'm due to start nursing training

Dad gets me a summer job in the sandwich factory

Where he drives deliveries with his drinking buddy,

Mrs's Dad   That joker, Terry.

Mrs   I'm appointed as 'top filling mixer'.

No production line for me

And packaged sandwiches were the future

In 1960.

She gets up, steps into her memory.

Then one hot day, it's egg mayonnaise

So I go into the big fridge

To collect a bucket of eggs

And in comes Terry.

Pulls the big fridge door shut

Says,

Terry (*white, cockney, Jack the Lad*)   Cwor it's hot. Wanna help me cool off?

Music changes to 'Mourn' by Corbin.

Mrs   I'm frozen to the spot.

Could have been a nurse,

Could have been a nun.

Sixteen years young.

I come out staring into a bucket of eggs

Shivering, bleeding, can't feel me legs

Ashamed.

Two weeks late.

Pregnant.

So Terry asks Dad for me hand

Dad buys a bottle of whisky

Mum kissed me

I sew a yellow dress

And up we all went down the registry office.

And since that day everybody just called me 'Mrs'

Terry Manners.

Mr   Mind your manners, Mrs!

Mrs He'd say.

As long as you mind yours, Mr!

I'd reply.

And he gets us this council flat all the way over in
Woolwich –

(*An aside.*) Might as well have moved to fucking France.

He carries me across the threshold and I giggle.

Mr I hope my Mrs ain't frigid.

Mrs I never laugh at that particular crack.

But I do learn to smile again,

Even learn to like him,

He was happy-go-lucky,

Says:

Mr I could love you, if you let me.

Mrs Gives up deliveries and starts painting and decorating
(*referring to the flat*)

Getting everything ready for our new baby.

Says he was –

Mr a good man really.

Not a lot of other white blokes would –

Mrs want me.

Mr And we look good together, don't we?

Milk and tea,

our baby will be the sugar.

You should take it nice and easy . . .

Mrs But our baby was born as still as a Sunday morning

And from that day

Terry never stops drinking

And I never stop thinking about Gabrielle

My angel,

And what she could have been,

And what she was doing now,

Above the clouds with Jesus . . .

Never did do that nursing training . . .

My dear old mum nursed me until

I went back to work at the sandwich factory

And all the girls gave me fags and made me sweet tea

'So, so, sorry . . .'

I hardly let Terry touch me after that

I only had to look at him and he froze.

I'd stay up late to avoid it

Watch the box (*an aside*) any old shit . . .

Years went by with Terry down the pub

And me sitting on the sofa,

Stroking the cats and staring at the sci-fis on the silver screen . . .

And one day the Evangelicals come knocking at the door

Church Elder One   Come to a Sunday Celebration?

Mrs   Thought, why not, what am I stuck in here for?

And I finally got pregnant with Michael

And Mr finally left me alone.

Years of affairs but I didn't care.

Got meself a nice desk job at British Telecom –

'Hailing frequencies open, Captain'.

Life was the girls at BT, my son and science fiction.

No worries, no plans, no expectations . . .

But when Michael left home I was stricken with grief again.

Couldn't get up for work anymore and they packed me in

I was due for retiring . . .

Scene Twelve: Shahana

DJ Son *plays The Jonzun Crew's version of 'Space Is the Place'.*

Mrs   I know.

There's something missing.

'Forgive me, Father for I have sinned

It's been years since my last confession.'

(*Excited confession.*) 1984:

Before the Evangelicals came to my door, before Michael was born . . .

I never imagined anyone could want me,

Love me,

Make love to me . . .

Until one day

A lady in a launderette offers me fabric softener with

Two drops of her own pressed lavender

And a smile that says –

Shahana *is a British-South-Asian musician from Lancashire, rich Blackburn or Accrington accent, nomad, free spirit, laid back.*

Shahana I handle delicates with care.

Mrs And somewhere between slow soak and fast spin

Everything feels washable and new.

In the launderette now. Animation of washing machines, soap suds and space . . .

The launderette was my sanctuary,

That's one place Mr would never follow me.

The men who did come in with their black bin bags

Always look a little found out

Shahana Huddled over their smalls

Hoping no one sees their white streaks and brown skids,

Ashamed of their own fluids . . .

Mrs Shahana was as easy as her name and the Lancashire rain.

She saw me watching her and asks

Shahana Want a bit?

Mrs Oh, sorry for staring I just . . .

Shahana Wondered if it makes a difference? It does, it really does.

Mrs And that's how it starts.

Shahana Have some lavender for your smalls.

Mrs Oh no, it's my husband's jumpers and me cat blankets!

Shahana Aw shame, well, let's make them all the fluffier shall we? . . .

Mrs We'd mostly meet on my morning off, a Monday . . .

Oh hello, Shahana . . . how are you?

Shahana Shattered.

Mrs   She'd been singing at some world festival or other

While I spent the weekend smiling at spillages on his shirts

Throwing bras in the yellow basket without a care in the world.

She said she finds

Shahana   the launderette relaxing. Watching the washing go round and round.

Mrs   Earth turning around the sun.

Shahana   And the heat in here is better than the leisure centre sauna and you don't have to deal with all the blokes asking about your tattoos.

Mrs   Shahana's got a lot of tattoos and piercings, purple streaks and a couple of teeth missing.

She looks like a pirate, and just as brave

And I only got one invitation.

She wanted to show me her van

Shahana   Correction: classic converted UPS delivery truck. Pine cabin inside – I did it all up meself.

Mrs   And I turned no more than ninety degrees before she kissed me,

Unfolded me

And stretched me out, like a clean sheet.

And I couldn't believe this was happening to me,

'Life begins at forty.'

There was so much water . . .

I never knew there could be so much water . . .

Like she was the force conducting the tides

And not the moon,

Not the moon at all . . .

And she rowed across my belly

Acting out all of this.

Like a pirate on the sea

She smuggled me.

I looked up from the deep

And on and on blindly

She crossed the ocean

Swelling inside me

Until she reached her island in the sun

And arched her back

And threw back her head

And sang out a YESSSSSSSSSS!

And crashed like waves upon my chest

Sshhhhhhhaaaaaaaaannnnaaaaaaahhh . . .

So that is what it is like,

I'd seen it in films but . . .

That is what it's like,

When it's real,

It is *so powerful*.

No wonder they keep trying to stop women from having them.

And me, I was just terrified of what it might do to me,

That if I exploded like her supernova

I'd never be able to put meself back together!

Shahana   Come on, Mrs, your turn.

Mrs   No. Shahana. Just hold me.

And she did. Gently. And I wanted nothing more.

Shahana   Correction: you don't feel you *deserve* anything more. You need to go home tonight, lock the bathroom door, light some candles and have a hot bath with lavender oil, lay back, let it all go and love yourself first, Mrs. No one else has a chance unless you do.

Mrs   I'll give it a try . . .

Shahana (*quoting* Star Wars)   'Try not. Do, or do not.'

Mrs (*finishing the quote, their little joke*)   'There is no try.'

Bye. (*Kisses* **Shahana** *goodbye.*)

But I went home to Mr instead

And said:

'It's time we got a washing machine.'

And I weren't being mean.

I just knew it was all over as soon as it began

Because when I looked up, Shahana was closing her eyes and mine were open wide.

'Hail Mary, full of grace

The Lord is with thee

Blessed art thee amongst women . . .'

Mondays especially I'd miss her

So instead of the launderette I'd visit the convent and sit with the old nuns

Momentarily sitting with the nuns in the convent.

And wonder if they'd ever had one,

And wonder what my life could have been

If I had a nun's habit instead of a smoking one,

And been married to gentle Jesus instead of Mr Terry Manners.

Who died on the toilet,

Cradling an empty bottle of whisky,

Like a baby.

Mrs' *action conveys the end of the online application.*

DJ Son   Here's another one of mine, a remix of Jamila Woods, 'Way Up' . . .

Shahana/Maryam's Song

As if at one of her gigs, **Shahana** *sings an acapella version of 'Way Up' by Jamila Woods. She sings in her own accent, she is easy with it. During the song,* **Maryam** *seamlessly takes over singing to herself.*[2] *Animation is projected of* **Maryam** *going into space, inspired by the song lyrics.*

DJ Son   Going back up with Sun Ra . . .

Scene Thirteen: Mrs Does the Crossword

Time has passed. **Mrs** *wears her glasses, does the crossword, listening to music, smoking her vape, a cloud of smoke, writing/ searching on the iPad – but not necessarily naturalistically. The crossword can be played out in the space.*

Mrs   Seven down

'Nerve ending of female pleasure. The Latin for shame.'

P space space E space space space.

---

2 Listen to the acoustic version of 'Way Up' by Jamila Woods. Available at https://www. youtube.com/watch?v=fGVW5T7R2U0 (accessed 14 February 2023).

Looks on the iPad for the answer, scanning her findings, reflected in the animation.

'As big as a phallus, on the inside:

The clitoris.

Twice as sensitive as the head of a penis

The only organ in the entire human body

Designed purely and only

For pleasure.'

I been googling.

Mrs *googles 'cut clitoris' on the iPad. She follows a film on YouTube.*

'200 million women and girls all over the world

Clipped, cut, sliced, sewn up,

Some left only with a hole the width of a matchstick

And on their wedding night, the groom takes a knife and . . .'

YouTube.

Overwhelmed.

Resumes crossword.

Seven down

P space space E space space space.

'The nerve ending of female pleasure'

(*Thinks.*) 'Pudenda'

'The Latin for shame.'

Mrs *suddenly thinks she hears* **Maryam** *in the toilet. Switches off the radio. No music. Silence for the only moment in the play.*

Mrs   Mary?

Maryam, you in there? . . .

You out there? . . .

Silence. **Mrs**, *a little afraid, turns on the radio again to fill the space.*

Eclipse, significance:

'Secrets, omens . . . Hidden emotions . . .'

'Something missing.'

'Turmoil, repressed.'

'Fear of failure,

Fear of success.'

Eclipse, science:

'A cosmic coincidence.'

What are the chances?

That I'd get invited to lunch, by Maxi.

DJ Son   'Sunday Morning' by Seven Davis Jr . . .

Scene Fourteen: Maxi[3]

Mrs   Maxi was younger than me, we used to work at BT.

We'd have such a laugh back then, but I retired and we drifted apart.

But recently Maxi got married to my butcher, Barry.

He's always decent to me.

Extra chipolatas since Mr died.

Started to feel there was a little bit of hope.

---

3 Thank you to Valentino Vecchietti of Intersex Equality Rights for consultation on this scene.

Company and cut-price pork chops,

They live above the shop.

One January Saturday when they were closing up,

Maxi invites me up for Sunday lunch.

Maxi *is in her fifties and young with it, Black, bold, full of life, power and joy.*

Maxi   Barry will be off dangling his maggots in the canal and I can't be bothered to do a roast just for meself. Come up and see me.

Mrs   I bought a nice bottle of wine and a box of Quality Street.

We chatted for hours.

Maxi said Barry the butcher was good to her: (*The women are tipsy.*)

Maxi   I got him trained! Now he's a damn good lover!

Mrs   I confided in Maxi on the sofa:

I took no pleasure in Mr what so ever

He might as well have been rubbing sand paper

He paid more attention to cutting in and decorating than he ever did to me.

Maxi   Poor you. Me and Barry lift off every Saturday night after *Britain's Got Talent*!

Mrs   I knew. Everybody knew. You could hear it half way up the high street.

Maxi   It's cos of my SUPERPOWER!

Mrs   Your what?

Maxi   Shall I tell you a story?

Mrs   Go on then.

Maxi   You sitting comfortable? When I was born, a doctor, named Money, stood at the end my mother's hospital bed and said (**Maxi** *plays* **Dr Money**, *upper-class, cold, arrogant, English surgeon*):

Dr Money   I'm afraid your 'daughter' has ambiguous genitalia. But we'll perform simple surgery, a quick cliterodectomy to cosmetically correct the clit –

Maxi's Mum (*who is from Jamaica*)   – but wait!

Dr Money   It is far too big to be a normal clitoris.

Maxi's Mum   Well, if I had given birt to a son who was hung like a donkey would we still be having dis conversation, Dr Money? No, I don't think so.

Maxi   And you know what he said?

Dr Money   It is deformed! If *that* was hanging off of your face you'd have a job . . .

Maxi   You'd have a job?!

Maxi, *outraged, goes off on one, fast, rapping along to the music.*

A nose job

A face-lift

A tummy-tuck

A cellulite suck

Botox pump

Breast implant

Buttock enhancement

Wax

Sack back and crack

Bum-hole bleach

Designer vagina

Vagina tightener

Labia reduction

Hymen restoration

Circumcision

Snip-excision

Clitordectomy

Infibulation

Any old genital mutilation

On or off the NHS

What's the difference?!

Beat. Back to the scene with **Maxi's Mum**. **Dr Money** *on the attack.*

Dr Money   Do you want her to have an abnormal life? How will she ever get a husband, be a *normal* wife – this child will grow up confused!

Maxi's Mum   Rewind, rewind, selector, come again . . . (**DJ Son** *rewinds the vinyl.*)

Maxi's Mum   Lemme get dis straight . . .

You wan fi tek my baby,

Guess what dem would have looked like,

If dem didn't look like what dem do

Mek dem look like something that dem don't

So it easier fi you to know what box to tick on what farm (*form*)?[4]

I tink *you* is de one dat is confuse, Dr Money!

---

4 Inspired by an interview with Jim Costich, in *Intersexion*, dir. Grant Lahood, 2011. Available at https://www.youtube.com/watch?v=QQdOp3COfSs (accessed 1 June 2018).

You can change de boxes on dat form ina yo hand,

But you nah go change my baby.

Put your scyalpel back ina yo pocket.

De Lawd mek no mistake!

I shall call her 'Maxi'.

And if she favour a bwoy, she can call himself Maxi same way. No problem.

Maxi (*as herself*)   They call me 'intersex' and I say too right I am into-sex! Heheyyyy!

I'm a Black Panther!

I got a superpower bigger than the King of Wakanda! (*Doing the 'Wakanda' greeting, larger than life now.*)

You can keep your vibranium!

I don't need no vibrator!

My body is natural and my orgasms are out of this wooooooooooooooorld STAR!

DJ Son *plays 'Cosmic Slop' by Funkadelic. Pause to take it all in.*

Mrs   Wow . . . Intersex . . .

Maxi   There's millions of us all over the planet. It's as common as being a redhead, but it's not connected, otherwise nuff Irish people would be hermaphrodites, innit? (*Laughs gently to herself at the thought.*) Seriously though, you never really know what's going with people inside, or down below. And I am one of the lucky ones. Cos most intersexys be much worse off than me. I read all about it in *To This Day!* magazine. Operating on people with no permission! Doctors lying to us, hiding us, humiliating us, shaming us. Secret surgeries, making out we got cancer, forcing us to be one way or another. Worldwide! It's a (*quoting*) 'gendercide!'[5] Doctors ain't supposed to play God, doctors ain't supposed to lie! Doctors ain't supposed to decide which bits of my privates look right to their eye! And get this, when I was eleven, yeah, the doctors wanted to operate on me *again*, but my mum says –

Maxi's Mum   Dey been messin wid Black women bodies since slavery days!

Chain and bit, speculum and whip. Anyone try fi touch you and we'll sue!

Maxi   And I got the balls to do it! Two, still on the inside doing just fine. Yes!

Mrs   Bloody hell, Maxi, you never said . . .

Maxi   No one talked about it back in the day. But I found this online action group. First off Barry didn't want me to get involved. Didn't want everyone knowing. I said (*to* **Barry**, *really going for him*) I'm not exactly going on *Loose Women*, Baz, its only a website! But he says: (**Barry** *is slow, kind, lumbering, cockney.*)

Barry   Let's just keep our sex life 'tween you and me, we only just got married, Maxi.

Maxi   It ain't about sex, Barry, it's about (*precisely quoting something she has read*) 'bodily integrity'.

Barry   Eh?

Maxi   Anyway, he's come around now.

Mrs   Has he?

Maxi   He's much more open-minded since I found him his G.

Mrs   His what?

---

5 Intersex activist Hida Viloria and others coined the term 'gendercide'. See https://hidaviloria.com/quoted-in-exc-washington-post-intersex-rights-movement-article/ (accessed 22 February 2019).

Maxi   His G-spot. I found it.

Mrs   Did you? Where?

Maxi   Up there. (*Simple gesture toward her bum.*)

Mrs (*half laugh half scream in horror*)   No! No! No!

Maxi (*gleefully*)   Yes! Yes, yes, Mrs! Every man's got a G-spot up his bum. Just most men are just too proud to let you at it, or too scared it might hurt, but when they do – wooooooooooooh! (*Singing.*) 'Free your behind and your mind will follow!' It ain't me you can hear screaming down the high street, Mrs, it's Barry, hahaaaa! He is so happy . . . (**Maxi** *is proud of herself.*)

Mrs   Really, Barry, up his bum? I'll never be able to look at his chipolatas the same way again. (*Pause for thought.*) Why the good Lord in his infinite wisdom chose to put a 'G-spot' in a man's bum-hole I will never know.

Maxi   Same reason he blessed us with a clitoris! You should count yourself lucky you got one! Have a holiday!

Mrs (*drifting for a moment*)   Yeah . . . (*Snapping back.*) Can't be that much of a sin then can it, Maxi? Enjoying your . . . self.

Maxi   What you on about, Mrs? I never understood your thing for religion. Priests, rabbis, urologists, gynaecologists – they're all the same to me. They just wanna control you! They wanna cut off my beautiful big clit! But you wanna see us on a Saturday after *Britain's Got Talent*! (*Beat.*) This chicken's dry. You having that stuffing?

DJ Son   That was 'Cosmic Slop' by Funkadelic. And here's Lyman, taking us down 'Joy Road' . . .

Mrs   As Maxi tucks into the remains of my plate I contemplate all it means for me . . .

Mrs   My mind wanders to all the hours I spent with the Evangelicals . . . Trying not to sneeze . . . Praying for the missionaries smuggling Bibles into communist China. I wondered if there were any ladies left in Beijing, toddling along on their tiny little feet, stumps, two inches wide. Men found their tangled toes attractive apparently, even under rotting bandages. (*Exhaling in disgust, distress.*) I wondered if anyone in China ever prayed for me.

'Pray for me . . .'

Maxi (*who has been watching* **Mrs**)   You all right, old girl?

Mrs   Sorry, where's my manners, I am forgetting myself. Whatchusay?

Maxi   You're drifting off a lot lately. You OK? . . .

Mrs   I don't think so, Maxi. I don't think I am . . .

DJ Son   'Peroration Six', Floating Points.

Scene Fifteen: The GP

Mrs   Me husband died

And it's taken my whole life

But, doctor

I've never had one

And I want one

Before I die . . .

My orgasm has got to be out there

Somewhere!

I know you all think I'm losing it

That I'm some kind of a . . . space cadet

And you might just be right about that!

So one last job for you, doctor

I'll be needing a medical certificate

To prove I am fit for travel.

I'm going away.

Scene Sixteen: The Plan

Mrs *is hurriedly packing whilst reading from* **Maryam**'s *stars project book, as if it is an instruction manual.* **Mrs**'s *speech is directed at 'Cat'. Fragments of animation drawn from the project book are projected as* **Mrs** *is trying to piece together her plan. The animation could be fragments that we have seen throughout the play, running through the scene and then climax at the end.*

Mrs   There is three things they don't tell you about space travel. One:

Maryam *reappears to* **Mrs**, *spirit-like.*

Maryam   It is extremely painful.

Mrs   Up there

Your body is a blissful skin bag of sinews and bones

Floating freeeeeee

But when you land home

The force

Is like a car crash –

I'm not talking whiplash

I mean every part of you feels crushed

And you can spend the rest of your life killing pain.

Maryam   Gravity is a grave.

No one is supposed to know.

Mrs   Disabled astronauts ain't the poster NASA wants to sell ya!

But that don't bother me . . . we're only able-bodied *temporarily*

Cos the other thing they don't tell you about travelling to space is . . .

When you're up there, the orgasms are out of this world!

Hahahahahahaha . . .

Mrs *hears 'Cat' in her head, 'What?'*

I know, Cat, that could be an 'alternative fact'

But it is one I am prepared to believe

Cos think about it

Where else do all the orgasms go?

All that energy!

All that power!

Must go somewhere?!

'The Earth moved!'

'I saw stars!' – 'Shooting stars!'

Ain't that what people say?

'Yes! Yes! Yes!'

There's nothing down here for the likes of me and

The likes of Mary . . .

(*Remembering* **Shahana**.) 'Love *yourself* first, Mrs . . . There is no try.'

And Maxi's right an' all –

I need a holiday!

One way.

A mission,

To have a '*petite mort*' before I die!

To come and go!

Perhaps sometimes to climax you gotta go that far!

And I ain't bothered about the pain landing back cos I plan to stay in space.

I seen enough saucers flying past my head to last me a lifetime down here

Give me one last pleasure

For all my trauma,

Let me fly!

'Spexit'.

Sound of an email pinging in an inbox. **Mrs** *is so excited!*

THE REPLY!

(*Reading the email optimistically.*) 'Dear Mrs Manners,

'We regret to inform you that you are ineligible for the government's "Spexit" relocation space flight. Priority is given to migrants, refugees from majority-Muslim countries and those still awaiting compensation from the Windrush Generation.'

Charming!

And to trump it all:

'We know that this will come as a further disappointment but the Virgin Luxury Space Holiday Travel Programme is only eligible for those aged under twenty-five.'

Pause. Disappointment. Perhaps a puff on her vape.

Maryam   You missed number three!

Mrs *looks in* **Maryam***'s stars book again.*

Mrs   The third thing they don't tell you about space travel is . . .

Maryam   There is more technology in a modern-day washing machine

Than the Sputnik that took the rocket dog to heaven

All on his own in 1957.

Mrs   HAIL MARY!

I got a washing machine

and a fridge!

Mrs *ends packing by putting the urn in the fridge. Entering a trance-like state, wide eyes, music gets louder, building to the climax!*

One small step

For a woman.

I'll boldy go

To *inner* space.

I shall

Shut

My

Eyes.

Tight.

I'll take the Gs

Dare

To forget myself

And remember

Who I am![6]

I will be afraid

No more. NO MORE!

---

6 Thank you to Sue Mayo for this line!

My name is: NORMA MONAGHAN but you can call me NOMMO!

My name is Norma Monaghan and I am coming HOME OHHHHHHH – YES!

MAY THE FORCE BE WITH *ME*!

MAY THE FORCE BE WITH YOU!

MAY THE FORCE BE WITH US AAAAAAAALL!

MY SUN! MY SON! HAIL FREQUENCIES OPEN!

Mrs *shuts her eyes. Dances wildly, as if she is inside a super-fast washing-machine cycle, until the end of the track which stops suddenly. Blackout. Breathing into the silence for three beats.* **DJ Son** *plays 'Scudd Books', the track from the opening. Mirror ball? Club night/star lights.*

DJ Son   Thanks for listening. But remember, this is just the beginning. See you on the dance floor down at (*whichever theatre/venue we are playing in*) 'til 2 a.m. Night's called *STARS* – a celebration of pleasure. Open to all. Entry is free.

A community chorus of women and non-gender-conforming technicians in jump suits burst on stage, transforming the space, collectively constructing the rocket, somehow. Alternatively the construction could combine projected animation and or motion capture, with the help of the audience. The women dress **Mrs**/*Norma Monaghan in the Nommo costume and mask from the opening. She takes the goldfish bowl, now a space helmet, and gets into the rocket. During this the concluding credits of the show are projected, animated in* **Maryam**'s *handwriting. The show transforms into a club night – a celebration of pleasure.*